Tropical Birds
Stencil Designs

Soraia Gebara José

DOVER PUBLICATIONS
Mineola, New York

Bibliographical Note

Tropical Birds Stencil Designs is a new work, first published by Dover Publications, Inc., in 2001.

DOVER *Pictorial Archive* SERIES

This book belongs to the Dover Pictorial Archive Series. You may use the designs and illustrations for graphics and crafts applications, free and without special permission, provided that you include no more than ten in the same publication or project. (For permission for additional use, please write to Permissions Department, Dover Publications, Inc., 31 East 2nd Street, Mineola, N.Y. 11501.)

However, republication or reproduction of any illustration by any other graphic service, whether it be in a book or in any other design resource, is strictly prohibited.

Library of Congress Cataloging-in-Publication Data

José, Soraia Gebara.
    Tropical birds stencil designs / Soraia Gebara José.
        p. cm. — (Dover pictorial archive series)
    ISBN 0-486-41719-0 (pbk.)
        1. Stencil work—Themes, motives. 2. Birds in art. 3. Birds—Tropics. I.
Title. II. Series.
    NK8655 .J67 2001
    745.7'3—dc21

                                                                                        00-066007

Manufactured in the United States of America
Dover Publications, Inc., 31 East 2nd Street, Mineola, N.Y. 11501

PUBLISHER'S NOTE

Bird motifs have been a perennial favorite among artists and decorators of all kinds. In this all-new collection, artist and naturalist Soraia Gebara José presents 118 bird stencils inspired by the extraordinary winged creatures of her homeland, Brazil. The birds range from the minuscule hyacinth visorbearer to the towering jabiru; from the musical white-eared puffbird to the talkative blue-fronted parrot; and from the fruit-eating Guianan red-cotinga to the most powerful bird of prey in the world, the harpy eagle. Some of these birds are extinct, some are threatened, some are thriving; but all have left an indelible mark on the landscape of their South American homeland.

Harpy Eagle
(*Harpia harpyja*)

American Pygmy Kingfisher
(*Chloroceryle aenea*)

Ringed Kingfisher
(*Ceryle torquata*)

5

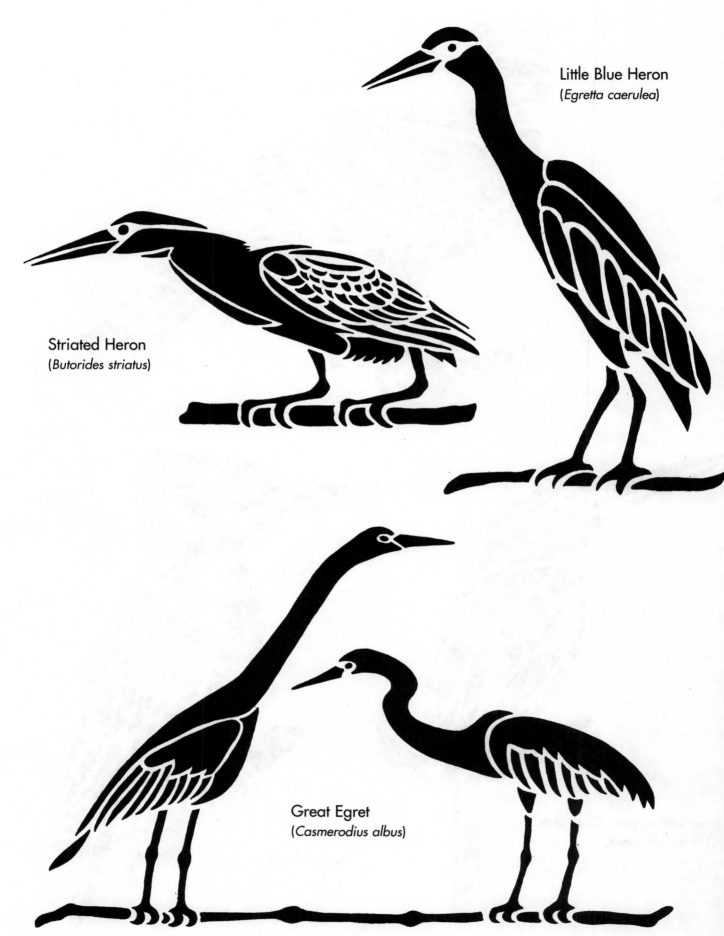

Little Blue Heron
(*Egretta caerulea*)

Striated Heron
(*Butorides striatus*)

Great Egret
(*Casmerodius albus*)

6

White-eared Puffbird
(*Nystalus chacuru*)

Jabiru
(*Jabiru mycteria*)

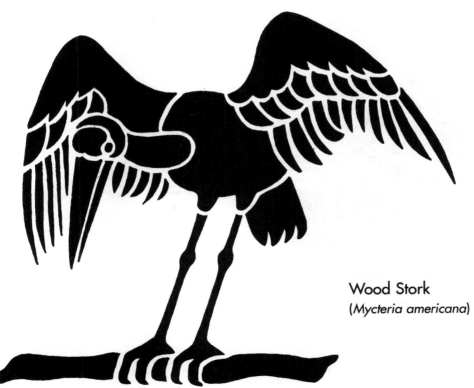

Wood Stork
(*Mycteria americana*)

7

White-naped Jay
(*Cyanocorax cyanopogon*)

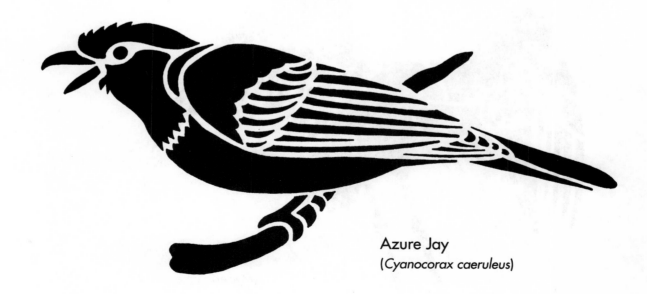

Azure Jay
(*Cyanocorax caeruleus*)

Curl-crested Jay
(*Cyanocorax cristatellus*)

Plush-crested Jay
(*Cyanocorax chrysops*)

Banded Cotinga
(*Cotinga maculata*)

White-winged Cotinga
(*Xipholena atropurpurea*)

Swallow-tailed Cotinga
(*Phibalura flavirostris*)

Guianan Red-Cotinga
(*Phoenicircus carnifex*)

Crimson Fruitcrow
(*Haematoderus militaris*)

Purple-throated Fruitcrow
(*Querula purpurata*)

Red-ruffed Fruitcrow
(*Pyroderus scutatus*)

Amazonian Umbrellabird
(*Cephalopterus ornatus*)

Hooded Berryeater
(*Carpornis cucullatus*)

Guianan Cock-of-the-Rock
(*Rupicola rupicola*)

13

Dusky-legged Guan (*Penelope obscura*)

Black-fronted Piping-Guan (*Pipile jacutinga*)

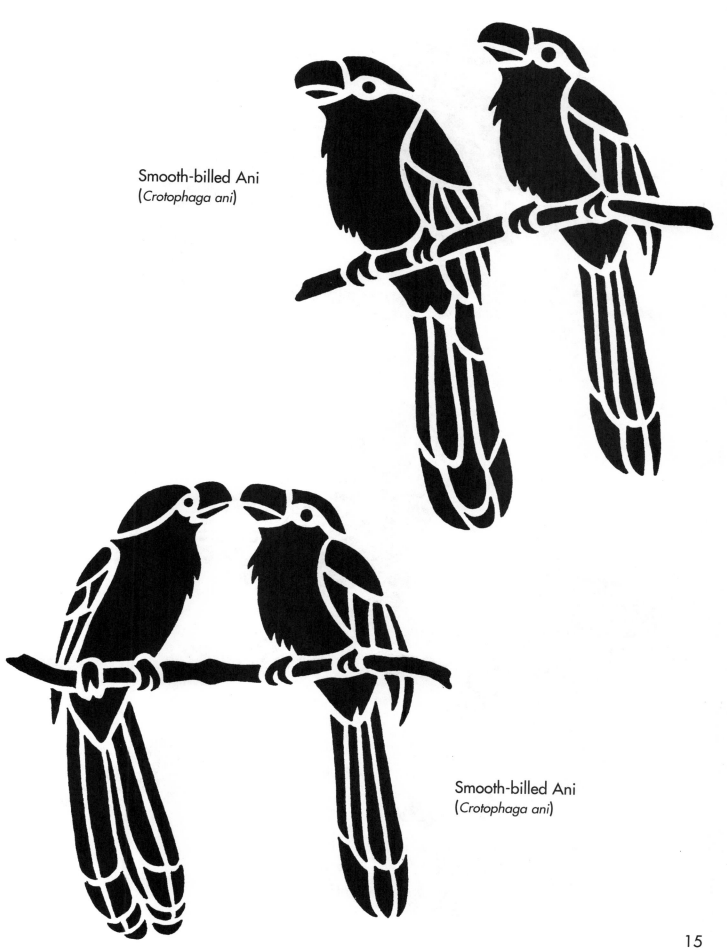

Smooth-billed Ani
(*Crotophaga ani*)

Smooth-billed Ani
(*Crotophaga ani*)

Swallow-Tanager
(*Tersina viridis*)

Diademed Tanager
(*Stephanophorus diadematus*)

Green-headed Tanager
(*Tangara seledon*)

Seven-colored Tanager
(*Tangara fastuosa*)

Seven-colored Tanager
(*Tangara fastuosa*)

Azure-shouldered Tanager
(*Thraupis cyanoptera*)

Brazilian Tanager
(*Ramphocelus bresilius*)

Fawn-breasted Tanager
(*Pipraeidea melanonota*)

Magpie Tanager
(*Cissopis leveriana*)

Great-billed Seed-Finch
(*Oryzoborus maximiliani*)

Lesser Seed-Finch
(*Oryzoborus angolensis*)

Antillean Euphonia
(*Euphonia musica*)

19

Red-cowled Cardinal
(*Paroaria dominicana*)

Red-crested Cardinal
(*Paroaria coronata*)

Yellow Cardinal
(*Gubernatrix cristata*)

20

Hooded Siskin
(*Carduelis magellanica*)

Rufous-tailed Jacamar
(*Galbula ruficauda*)

Great Jacamar
(*Jacamerops aurea*)

Blue-and-white Swallow
(*Notiochelidon cyanoleuca*)

White-banded Swallow
(*Atticora fasciata*)

22

Troupial (*Icterus icterus*)

Shiny Cowbird (*Molothrus bonariensis*)

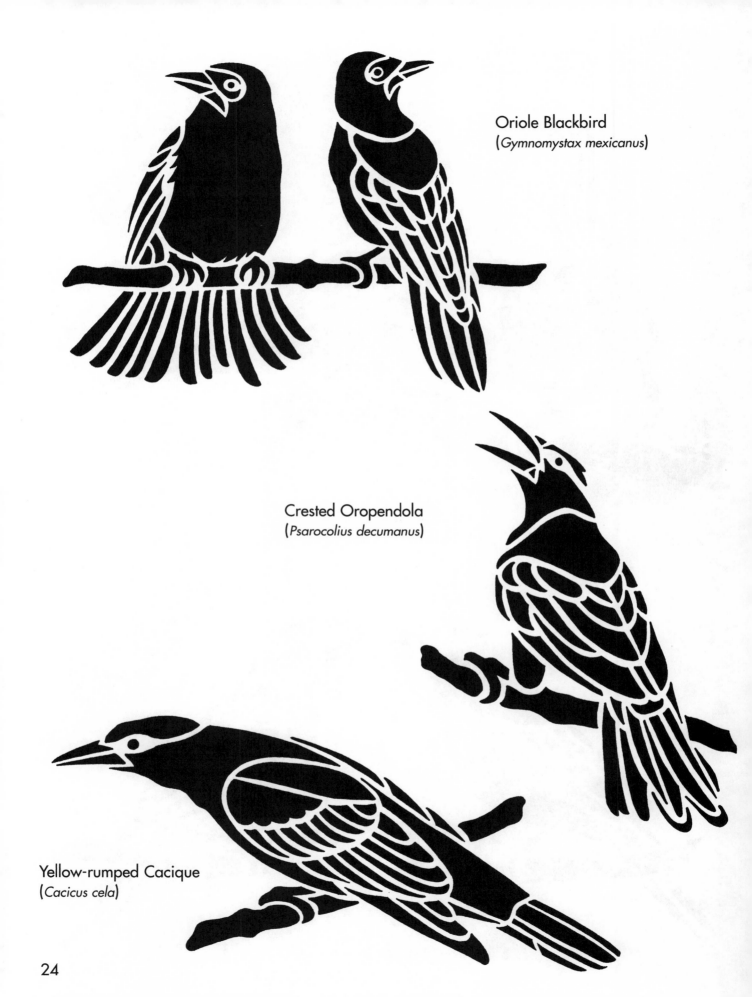

Oriole Blackbird
(*Gymnomystax mexicanus*)

Crested Oropendola
(*Psarocolius decumanus*)

Yellow-rumped Cacique
(*Cacicus cela*)

24

Rufous-capped Motmot
(*Baryphthengus ruficapillus*)

Blue-crowned Motmot
(*Momotus momota*)

Rufous-vented Ground-Cuckoo
(*Neomorphus geoffroyi*)

Robust Woodpecker
(*Campephilus robustus*)

Red-necked Woodpecker
(*Campephilus rubricollis*)

Greater Flamingo
(*Phoenicopterus ruber*)

Red-headed Manakin
(*Pipra rubrocapilla*)

Opal-crowned Manakin
(*Pipra iris*)

Wire-tailed Manakin
(*Pipra filicauda*)

27

Blue-crowned Manakin
(*Pipra coronata*)

Band-tailed Manakin
(*Pipra fasciicauda*)

White-fronted Manakin
(*Pipra serena*)

Black-capped Manakin
(*Piprites pileatus*)

Blue Manakin
(*Chiroxiphia caudata*)

Pin-tailed Manakin
(*Ilicura militaris*)

Blue-bellied Parrot
(*Triclaria malachitacea*)

Red-browed Parrot
(*Amazona rhodocorytha*)

Scaly-headed Parrot
(*Pionus maximiliani*)

White-bellied Parrot
(*Pionites leucogaster*)

Vinaceous Parrot
(*Amazona vinacea*)

Red-spectacled Parrot
(*Amazona pretrei*)

Blue-fronted Parrot
(*Amazona aestiva*)

Golden-tailed Parrotlet
(*Touit surda*)

Blue-fronted Parrot
(*Amazona aestiva*)

Blue-winged Parrotlet
(*Forpus xanthopterygius*)

Golden Parakeet
(*Aratinga guarouba*)

Jandaya Parakeet
(*Aratinga jandaya*)

Nanday Parakeet
(*Nandayus nenday*)

Monk Parakeet
(*Myiopsitta monachus*)

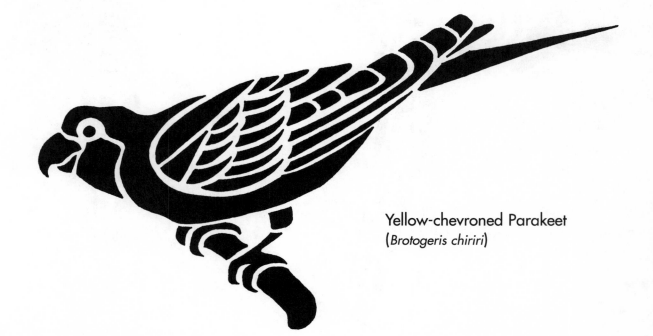

Yellow-chevroned Parakeet
(*Brotogeris chiriri*)

Sun Parakeet
(*Aratinga solstitialis*)

Peach-fronted Parakeet
(*Aratinga aurea*)

White-eared Parakeet
(*Pyrrhura leucotis*)

Lear's Macaw
(*Anodorhynchus leari*)

Scarlet Macaw
(*Ara macao*)

Scarlet Macaw
(*Ara macao*)

Red-and-green Macaw
(*Ara chloropterus*)

Hyacinth Macaw
(*Anodorhynchus hyacinthinus*)

Spix's Macaw
(*Cyanopsitta spixii*)

37

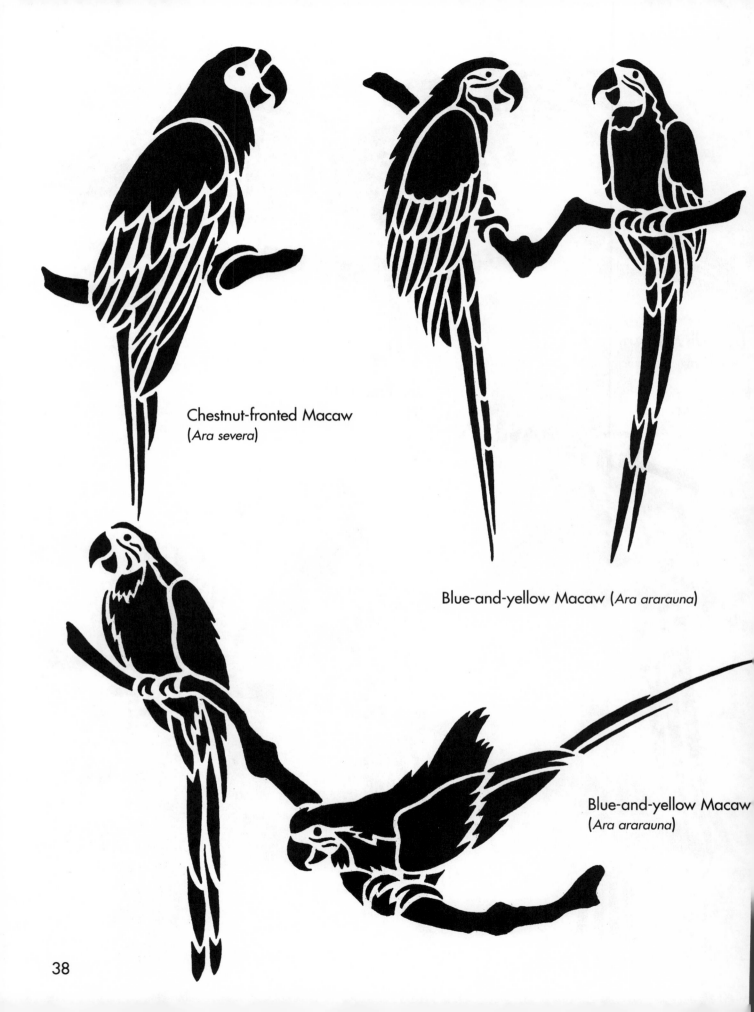

Chestnut-fronted Macaw
(*Ara severa*)

Blue-and-yellow Macaw (*Ara ararauna*)

Blue-and-yellow Macaw
(*Ara ararauna*)

Channel-billed Toucan
(*Ramphastos vitellinus*)

Red-breasted Toucan
(*Ramphastos dicolorus*)

Toco Toucan (*Ramphastos toco*)

Black-necked Aracari
(*Pteroglossus aracari*)

Yellow-ridged Toucan
(*Ramphastos culminatos*)

Spot-billed Toucanet
(*Selenidera maculirostris*)

Black-winged Stilt
(*Himantopus himantopus*)

Brown Booby
(*Sula leucogaster*)

Scarlet Ibis
(*Eudocimus ruber*)

Roseate Spoonbill
(*Ajaia ajaja*)

Roseate Spoonbill
(*Ajaia ajaja*)

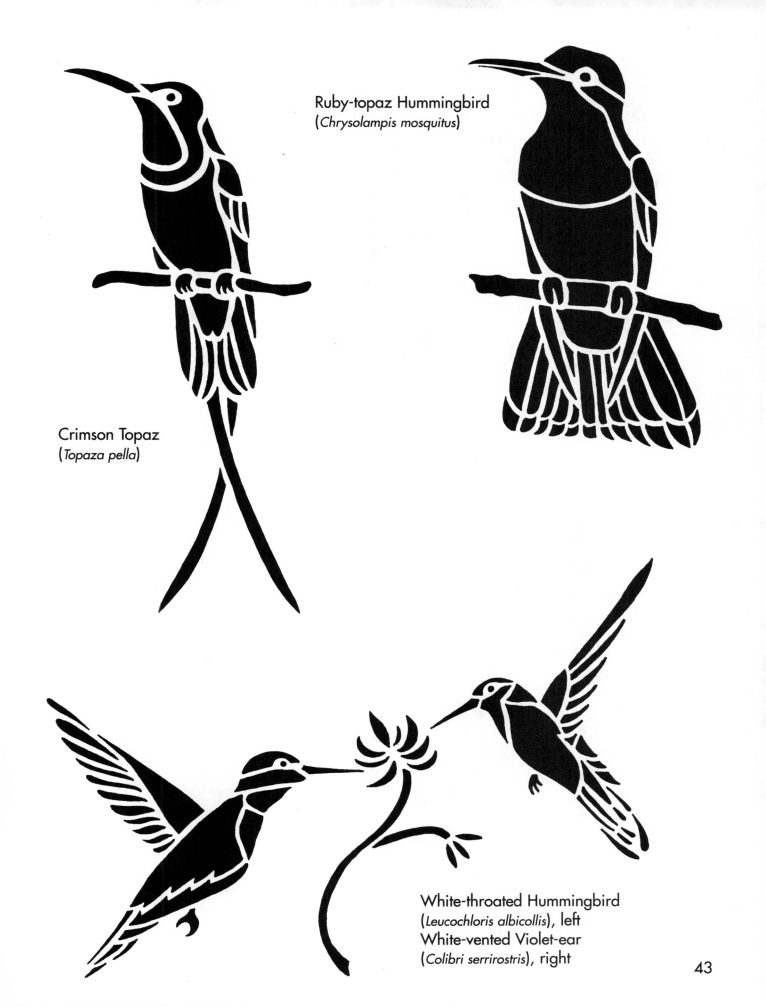

Ruby-topaz Hummingbird
(*Chrysolampis mosquitus*)

Crimson Topaz
(*Topaza pella*)

White-throated Hummingbird
(*Leucochloris albicollis*), left
White-vented Violet-ear
(*Colibri serrirostris*), right

43

Hyacinth Visorbearer
(*Augastes scutatus*)

Plovercrest
(*Stephanoxis lalandi*)

Brazilian Ruby
(*Clytolaema rubricauda*)

Musician Wren
(*Cyphorhinus aradus*)

White-tailed Trogon
(*Trogon viridis*)

Rufous-bellied Thrush
(*Turdus rufiventris*)

Rufous-brown Solitaire
(*Cichlopsis leucogenys*)

Great Kiskadee
(*Pitangus sulphuratus*)

Royal Flycatcher
(*Onychorhynchus coronatus*)

Many-colored Rush-Tyrant
(*Tachuris rubrigastra*)

Index of Common Names